AT THE WINDOW, SILENCE

Kenneth Pobo

Fernwood
PRESS

At the Window, Silence

©2025 by Kenneth Pobo

Fernwood Press
Newberg, Oregon
www.fernwoodpress.com

All rights reserved. No part may be reproduced for any commercial purpose by any method without permission in writing from the copyright holder.

Printed in the United States of America

Cover and page design: Mareesa Fawver Moss
Cover image placed in the public domain by
   Rippl-Rónai Municipal Museum, Hungary

ISBN 978-1-59498-156-2

For Stan

Contents

Acknowledgments 9
Inside 13
   My Sister Agatha Can Fly 14
   Hector Husband 15
   I Visit Moma and Lunch with Frank O'Hara 16
   Found Picture 17
   Marriage and Canned Peaches 18
   Dad's Science 19
   Grace by the Piano 20
   Lovable Moptops 21
   A Hiker 22
   The Drop In 23
   Mars Changing Her Name 24
   Talking About Hinduism with Thoreau 25
   Antique Store Bette Davis 26
   Promises, Promises 27
   Chester, 12, Looks in the Mirror 28
   Cold Tapioca 29
   Old Salt 30
   Pompeii 31

- Geometry Teacher 32
- Post-Donald 33
- Hopkins in Doubt 35
- Cowardly Lion Now 36
- Men in Eve's Life 37
- Talking Snake 38
- Adam, a Week Before Dying 39
- Genesis Unexpurgated 40
- Judas Upgraded 41
- Loki 42
- Medusa and Men 43
- Hades Wants It All the Time 44
- Bloody Mary 45
- Woodrow Wilson 46

Outside 47
- New Seed Catalogues 48
- First Pansies 49
- Grapefruit 50
- Plan Without Lemons 52
- Elegy for a Calamondin 54
- Hepatica 55
- Trilliums 56
- Yellow Buddleia 57
- Fuschia 58
- I'm Misting 59
- Planting in the Rain 60
- Blue Himalayan Poppy 61
- Petunias 62
- Weeding Borders 63
- On Being Told Any Poet Who
  Writes About Flowers Is Safe 64
- Giant Hogweed 65
- Popillia Japonica 66

Rose After Eden 67
First Blossom 68
A Red Dahlia 69
A Show-and-Tell Dahlia 70
Belle of Barmera Dahlia 71
Sandia Rose Dahlia 72
I Like to See My Plants Naked 74
Adenium 75
Tall Mexican Sunflowers 76
Farfugium with Exclamation Point 77
Moonflower on the Porch 78
November Potatoes 79
Start of Spring 80
Mask and Garden 81
Ghost Garden 82

Title Index 83
First Line Index 87

Acknowledgments

"My Sister Agatha Can Fly"—*Smeuse* (England)
"Hector Husband"—*I Can Count To Ten*
"I Visit MOMA and Lunch with Frank O'Hara"—*Amarolla* (Cyprus)
"Found Picture"—*Floor Plan*
"Marriage and Canned Peaches"—*Rio Grande Review*, Moonstone Arts Press: *The Book of Micah* (chapbook)
"Dad's Science"—*Mobius*
"Grace by the Piano"—*Hashtag Queer*
"Lovable Moptops"—*The Lake* (England)
"A Hiker"—*Internet Void*
"The Drop In"—*Exeter Press*
"Mars Changing Her Name"—*Syzygy Poetry Journal*, Southern Arizona Press
"Talking Hunduism with Thoreau"—*Liturgical Credo*
"Antique Store Bette Davis"—*Arabesques*
"Promises, Promises"—*Leopardskin and Limes*
"Chester, 12, Looks in the Mirror"—*Hidden Oak*

"Cold Tapioca"—*Marathon*
"Old Salt"—*Enigma*
"Pompeii"—*The Muse*
"Geometry Teacher"—*The Toucan*
"Post-Donald"—*Carte-Blanche* (Canada)
"Hopkins in Doubt"—*Afterthought*
"Cowardly Lion Now"—*The Lake* (England)
"Men in Eve's Life"—*Silence To Speech: Women of The Bible Speak Out*
"Talking Snake"—*Tower Poetry* (Canada)
"Adam, a Week Before Dying"—*Some Words*
"Genesis Unexpurgated"—*Thirty-First Bird*
"Judas Upgraded"—*Adroitly Placed Word*
"Loki"—*Philadelphia Inquirer Online*
"Medusa and Men"—*The Courtship of Winds, Calligraphy with Ball* (chapbook) Encircle Press
"Hades Wants It All the Time"—*Centrifugal Eye*
"Bloody Mary"—*Blue Lake Review*
"Woodrow Wilson"—*Ink, Sweat and Tears* (England)
"New Seed Catalogues"—*Reedy Branch Review*
"First Pansies"—*Ghoti*
"Grapefruit"—*Sheila-Na-Gig*
"Plan Without Lemons"—*South Florida Poetry Journal*
"Elegy for a Calamondin"—*The Lake* (England)
"Hepatica"—*In Between Hangovers*
"Trilliums"—*Fleas on the Dog*
"Yellow Buddleia"—*A New Ulster* (Northern Ireland)
"Fuschia"—*Other Terrain* (Australia)
"Planting in the Rain"—*Juke Joint*
"I'm Misting"—*Poem2Day*

"Blue Himalayan Poppy" — *From East to West*
"Petunias" — *The Mantle*
"Weeding Borders" — *Verse-Virtual*
"On Being Told" — *The Lowell Pearl*
"Giant Hogweed" — *Verse-Virtual*
"Popillia Japonica" — *Epiphany Magazine*
"A Red Dahlia" — *Rue Scribe*
"A Show and Tell Dahlia" — *Brittle Star* (England)
"Belle of Barmera Dahlia" — *A New Ulster* (Northern Ireland)
"Sandia Rose Dahlia" — *Verse-Virtual*
"I Like to See My Plants Naked" — *The Lake* (England)
"Adenium" — *Fiction And Verse*
"Tall Mexican Sunflowers" — *Ishaan Literary Review*
"Farfugium with Exclamation Point" — *Poeming Pigeon*
"Moonflower on the Porch" — *Buenos Aires Review* (Argentina)
"November Potatoes" — *West Trade Review*
"Start of Spring" — *Brittle Star* (England)
"Mask and Garden" — *The Poet Magazine*
"Ghost Garden" — *Loch Raven Review*

Inside

My Sister Agatha Can Fly

Dad called her a princess,
and mom called her Elizabeth Taylorette.
She flew for the first time at nine.
I was eleven. They told me,
"If she can do it, so can you. Don't be lazy."
I had no answer. I was lazy.

One Christmas, I gave Agatha a book on Icarus,
hoping she'd fly too close to the sun.
I doubt she read it. Sometimes,

almost twenty years later, she drops in
from the sky. We eat graham crackers.
She flies home. I look down
at my bare feet, so rooted to the ground
that violets grow from my toes.

Hector Husband

At the foot of my boyhood bed,
a brown stuffed dog, Hector,
that I called my wife.
With a stuffed dachshund named Sandy,
we could have been a stick-figure
family on a car's back window.
My parents kept quiet,
Hector being a dog and all,
and not even a living dog.

After grade school it became clear
that no one would accept Hector
as my wife. Or husband.
Stupidly, I gave Hector away
to Goodwill, telling myself
that he would make another kid
so happy. A coward,

I never told Hector that we were over.
Polaroids of him and me fade
in my bureau. Sometimes
I take them out and feel a wind
blow through me
in our still house.

I Visit Moma and Lunch with Frank O'Hara

Cornflake sky falls into a bowl
of dream sometimes
when I awaken I turn to groggy Stan
and ask if he's so sure
that he doesn't have a soul—I've seen his soul—
I do tricks with it make it leap but Frank

you've come no one can see us
eating smelly sandwiches in the museum
paintings remember you fondly
you say the one thing you miss
more than sex
is a brisk Manhattan walk

on a brisk October day Bette Davis
rising from the Roosevelt Hotel roof
to moon Joan Crawford thanks

for lunching with me one more
living cigarette inhaled
deeply on a busy street dusk

Found Picture

A barren lilac,
a few trees beginning to leaf.

On the right-hand side
the date: Apr 63. Fourth grade,
Mrs. Hieronymous. Or miss?
Memory is a chalkboard,
no chalk, just an eraser.
In seven months I'd see
a real murder,
Jack Ruby killing Oswald,
my parents out. A Sunday.

My shoulders are back,
my suit jacket buttoned
in the middle,
one button only, pants dark
like muddy cinnamon.
Only us three in the frame.

It's like we're on a ledge,
completely unconcerned
that we may step badly
and fall. Everyone steps badly.
There's no choice.

Marriage and Canned Peaches

A picture of Mary's bleeding
heart hangs in their austere
living room. When we visit,
they turn on a game show
so loud that we must talk over it
while trying not to look
at the wall with the heart
beating against fading magenta.

When she brings us each
a bowl of cold canned peaches,
she says of him: We stopped
talking about thirty-five
years ago. She gives such
news like a weather report.
Sometimes he pipes in a remark.

After we leave, in our own home
when we try to touch each other,
Mary's face appears, still stricken.
We sit on opposite sides
of her sad eyes, then talk of work,

the moon trapped like a key
that broke in a lock.

Dad's Science

His integers got me
fuzzy—with dry ice steaming,

he was a Gomez Addams
who said he worked with a
spectrometer—that sounded like
the dark in our basement. While
I pretended to be Stonewall Jackson,

Twenty miles away
he mapped light. Mom and I never
asked for details. He would say work
was fine, fine after stepping in
our back door. Now

he sits beside an avocado tree
in the living room, asks
about my life four states away. Fine,

I say, my own maps as strange
to him as his were to me.

Grace by the Piano

Grace would come over for coffee,
sing, share Bible talk. Mom
accompanied her on songs
like "I Believe" or "Trees."
A high note could unhinge a door.

Suburban Chicago women,
mostly quiet, their pain
in deep cupboards. I barged in on
some truths if we got out
of school early.

Afternoon died into homework.
When my folks sold our house,
Grace's voice remained in the paint.
What did the new owners hear
when the lights turned off
and the house shook,
the picture window vibrating.

Lovable Moptops

I saw them first on Ed Sullivan.
The boys in fourth grade wanted
long hair. Dad, deadset against it,
slathered on Brylcreem,
kept me crew-cutted—
it mattered how you voted on
who is your favorite Beatle. George,
always George.

When they got psychedelic, I pondered
"All You Need Is Love." Half a century later,
love is a dying deer along a road.
Or something quaint taken down
from the attic. We serve hate
bottled water at dinner.

I program in "Piggies." They won,
the oinking too loud through most
any window. Expensive clothing
hides us.

It's been a hard day's night
on a planet where daybreak
didn't hear the alarm.

A Hiker

discovers a skeleton,
probably a woman,
after walking
from our road
into the state
park—authorities ask
about missing persons
over the past
several years
a half an hour
from where

we separate
your underwear
from mine
and Skype
with a friend
from Illinois.

The Drop In

When Li Bei drops in, and normally
we hate people who do that,
we drop everything—"He's here,

the great poet, we must welcome him."
He smells like cinnamon ferns,
flops down on our cat-scratched couch
and talks about death, how it's not so bad,
but sometimes you just have to see

a swiftly moving river again. Here
we have no river, only a red poppy
that dares to bend space
and time into one, at least

for a day or two. His mouth
drops open. Either the poppy
has caused both death and life
to stop for him—or he's parched.
It's both. I bring him cranberry

wine we got in Wisconsin,
a sweet, cheerful taste. After drinking it,
he disappears, no goodbye. Perhaps
a poem came to him, and
he couldn't wait to get it down—

or, he had a river to find,
water to cool his feet, a blue
heron to share it with.

Mars Changing Her Name

I got named after a war god.
People should call themselves
war gods as they specialize
in war. I'm sanguine,
my two moons,
Phobos and Deimos,
like a trowel and a spade,
dig the garden of space.

I get angry. How would you
like an asteroid to bop you on
the ass? I'd prefer
a gender-neutral name
like Chris. Planet Chris.
Someone you could call
when a storm leaps out
and you're scared.

Gossip from Uranus
says people want to colonize me.
I'd rather not be
a dinner table
with strangers deciding how
to turn me into cash. That might

make me a war god after all,
freezing out these visitors
who think I'm property,
who have signed deeds for hearts.

Talking About Hinduism with Thoreau

When I visit his little grave,
I ask him to return

with me to Pennsylvania—
he comes willingly to see

the twenty-first century up close.
Where else to go

but to a mall? He avoids
the food court, thinks he sees

Krishna in fluorescent lighting,
but it's only a reflection

of Super Mario. He vanishes—
I wave, let him go,

the grave clearly livelier
than such a place as this.

Antique Store Bette Davis

I riffle through photos
of old stars and politicians. Ah,
here's Bette Davis
in her forties or fifties—a movie
still, or is she walking
in Hollywood? A sweater

over her shoulders, she clenches
both hands, red mouth
boiling over. I buy the photo,
put it on my desk.
Like Catholics sometimes do
with favorite saints.

Promises, Promises

Dear Dionne Warwick, that champagne
bubbles in a crystal-glass voice,
the just-right intonation. Sometimes

I fall into the vinyl groove,
the red Scepter label spinning
like a fan behind my eyes.

Dionne meets me, serves me a slice
of piping song. Today
she's singing about where promises
can lead.

Promises are mud.
They stick to your shoes.
They make a mess when you track them
into the house. Yet
you hope they aren't mud

but a porch where you sit
with someone who also watches
hummingbirds dart
to the plastic red feeder.
They never stay. That's often

the way with promises. Dart and go.
Or watch them teeter at the edge,
not falling,
lighter than the heaviest vowel.

Chester, 12, Looks in the Mirror

Grandma calls me *pudgy*.
Mom says that soon
I'll be *filling out*.

Am I a balloon?
I could float above the roof.

I'm a collection of names.
At school,
when I'm not called *faggot*,
I'm called by my last name,
called by my first at home.
If those names were tape,
I'd peel them off
and go my way,
nameless,

a bright red balloon
that might pop.

Cold Tapioca

When I told Dun Dunt that
I had fallen in
love, he served me cold tapioca.
With magic powers. I became

a large house. A new family
moved into me, opening
my doors and windows.
Two kids clattered up my stairs.
The parents bickered about where
to put the venus flytrap. I made
a frumpy house. I flopped
at being in love—whenever
I promised eternity, my cobra
watch spit numbers back.

Maybe this new love would be
different. Dun Dunt said
go slowly—summer's door stays
open for three months.
Water seeping through a clogged drain,
I do go slowly. Maybe

someday we'll be ready, overtake
each other's houses, keys bent,
butter locks melting.

Old Salt

We ask to take his picture,
then watch the sun fall,
charred red waves, walk

around Key West, pass him
again, his cap a ship
heading somewhere full

of mimosa and coconuts—wind
pushes him just
over the sky.

Pompeii

Your beauty is like a calendar
with August missing. I said
if you're late again, I'll drop you
in the Delaware River. You
were on time. I called you darling

when a horse from an ancient farm
showed up at my door. You didn't
say darling back. I waited for
a century to crumble
like the gardenia I pinned on
my prom date. You're cold,

and I'm Pompeii sniffing
a smoking mountain.

Geometry Teacher

I've always taught that the shortest distance
between two points

is
a
straight
line.

Such a truth never made me
happy, so I drank
and downed cylindrical pills.

Eventually the principal,
Mrs. Adair, fired me,
a bad example.
I became a rhombus—
until my lines

broke. Even
triangles avoid me.

Post-Donald

After we broke up, Donald met a reporter
he married in Madrid, had three kids. For years
I'd get Christmas cards, "Hope you had a great year
and were in many plays, Donald." I did some plays,
won no Tony's, had a good face. Remember

the Tulli gum girl in the late 70s? That's me!
"A blast of hoocheekoo! in every chew."
That gig lasted almost five years. I almost married Troy.
Daddy, wheelchair-bound in the Friendly Waters
Retirement Community since Mom died, freaked.

"You won't marry that Black guy. I'll die first."
I might've married him, but marriage
felt like a show that closed after a dozen performances.
The empty theater, wickets shut. Sexually,
I like women better,

maybe. Some women. Men often rush,
like I'm who they channel surf through
on the way to see the Giants snuff the Packers.
Not Donald. Considerate, he probably
wearied of my good-girl schtick, didn't lay me

for our first five years. Heavy petting, yes. Acting
took me everywhere from L.A. to London,
kept us apart. Now I'm in Ft. Wayne, Indiana,
left overpriced New York. Mostly my roles
are old grans. This week I'm performing

Nanny in *The Effect of Gamma Rays*.
Each night I drive back to my ranch house,
sing along with old songs, the Fifth Dimension
my favorite group—the dawning
of the Age of Aquarius. Lights out.

Hopkins in Doubt

I love a man, Lord, and don't know
what you would have me do. You call

me to celibacy. I need touch—
would you cast me out? That would

do little good. Where would I turn?
The Apostle Paul said that we

should marry rather than burn.
Why should I do either? I can't run

to or from you. Any tree
needs rain—I wither in your sun.

Cowardly Lion Now

I quit Oz after eight months,
hated paperwork, wanted to be
back in the forest
where I ate too much.

No one called me King.

I guarded secrets of ferns,
rescued flies from spider webs,
sired kittens that left me
as I had left my mother.
I shake my mane, fully gray,
lap starlight from
a marshy pond.

When I see my face in the water,
I know this world
isn't black and white.
Color keeps sneaking in.

Men in Eve's Life

Genesis 3:16

1.

He complains endlessly about how tired he is
of working the land. I comfort him
but it gets old. Does he think having babies
without a doctor or nurse, even a midwife, is easy?
The kids give me many butts to clean.
Sometimes I'd like to sit under a tree
and do nothing. So would he.
We could hold hands and be
naked like in the old days. Long ago.
When we were friends as well as lovers.

2.

Look, I made a mistake. I didn't think
a snake would lie. Most just crawled
around, colorful ropes. And I ate.
From one tree. I didn't make the rule—you did.
Had I made rules for you, I wonder how long
before you broke them? It's not so easy.
I have no command over angels. I can't open
and close gardens at my whim. It's enough
just to feed kids and calm Adam.
Survival is a tiny slender thread.

Talking Snake

Did Eve find the snake's
voice seductive?
Authoritative? Maybe
it sounded like a pubescent boy,
voice breaking. What if

Adam had gone walking
instead? Eve,
seeing him return, thinking
gosh, he's naked,
what could that mean,
I'd better hide.

Adam, a Week Before Dying

I've spent my life blaming her—
if only, if only. She shrugs,
has babies, calls me fussy.

We never talk about
when we walked naked.
I can tell she thinks

about those times, maybe
craving a delicious taste
she'll never savor again.
Trees used to make our lunch,
bushes set our table.

Hardass God! One mistake
and you're out! Apologies
only rile him. Did we

apologize? Joy bored us
enough to take a risk.
It wasn't her fault. The snake
found her first. And why blame
the snake? Such eloquence!

Death is near. Where will
God put us when we die?

Why do our kids never ask
about our pasts?

Genesis Unexpurgated

On the first day
God created a telescope. On the second
God created a microscope. On the third
God created a guitar. On the fourth
God created us. On the fifth
God regretted yesterday. On the sixth
God wrote a poem. God kept
the seventh day open—for revision.

Judas Upgraded

Dante's betrayers faced horror—
Judas had to spend eternity
in Satan's mouth, clearly
quite a pickle to be in over
thirty silver pieces. Maybe

it showed greed (or did he need cash
for a sick family member?)
and bad judgment. Jesus
knew he was going to die—
Judas didn't change anything.

Let's get some fireproof tongs
to pull him out. He's suffered enough.
If Satan needs his mouth refilled,
why not fry up some oil executives?

Maybe Judas, freed,
will email Jesus and say,
Hey, I goofed. Sorry.

Loki

A trickster, I dwell in surprise—
what do I care if you like me?
Half of me is truth. Half is lies.

Look closely and don't criticize.
Changing shape is my destiny.
A trickster, I dwell in surprise,

so don't trust what's before your eyes.
I appear, disappear quickly.
Half of me is truth. Half is lies.

You want to be what you despise,
yet you know you can't be this free.
A trickster, I dwell in surprise,

am most happy when in disguise.
Be a fish, a mare, he or she.
Half of me is truth. Half is lies—

like the darkness that dawn denies,
none can stopper my energy—
a trickster, I dwell in surprise.
Half of me is truth. Half is lies.

Medusa and Men

From the tops of stairs
in a mall, nabbing me in
a rearview mirror, or

at the gym when I'm riding
a stationary bike—they think
I don't catch them staring.
I am a scene seen.

When they turn to stone,
what else to do but laugh?
How boring they are,
like colorless pebbles.

Hades Wants It All the Time

Hades wants it all the time. I think
about glads tilting against
marigolds, have tried to keep
a tidy house here in hell,
burning boots marking floors.
Creeps, cowards, and traitors
keep us company. I want my mom.
Has she forgotten me?

Or has Eros shot her too, left her
pining for some goofball
so she forgets to sing seeds awake
and look for me.

Bloody Mary

Heretics,
a true danger, worse than murder,
had to be set ablaze—she thought
she was just. Even she has a story—
a dad who sometimes
wanted her dead, a mom
tossed away like a torn sweater,
a brother who tried to sabotage her,
a husband who found her blah.

Sometimes the terrible
have aches
that never go away.

Woodrow Wilson

For my ninth birthday
my grandparents gave me a book
of presidents which stopped at JFK.
I often leafed through it, skimming
the few paragraphs on each,
which never criticized—
they all had magic
it would seem. But #28—

I taped a paper over his face.
He looked like he could dash out
of the binding and eat me alive.
Woodrow Wilson. A stern-faced
Princeton prof. I later learned
he worked to the point of strokes
to get countries to talk
instead of fight. Yet ramped up
segregation, admiring
Birth of a Nation
for its Ku Klux crapping.

The book yellows in the basement
under cat litter and a few
cracked 45s. Wilson, is that you
I hear wandering up the stairs?
In your tidy suit? Your white sheet?

Outside

New Seed Catalogues

I pluck leaves
from the car vent,
toss beauty onto
the driveway, check
the mailbox, stuffed
with seed catalogues.
Daylily. Just saying the word
wraps me in a peace quilt.
Maybe one catalogue will
offer hepaticas. Spring
bellows from tiny flowers,
bubbles up in dreams,
though frost
will surely come tonight.

First Pansies

of the year! A flat for twenty bucks.
Three days ago, the first crocus, yellow.
Two days ago, the first snowdrop, white.
Today, pansies, a color hotel,
and I need a room. In junior high,

kids often called me a pansy.
I tiptoed on glass shards,
covered my head. Did they
fear color? Variety? I have
the perfect place to plant them,

to grow the eighth-grade boy
I should have been: a color-sizzling kid,
able to brave cold weather,
not the one slammed against a locker,
training my face to lose all expression.

Grapefruit

1.

Squirt me in the eye again
you ruddy thing
and I'll bounce you like a watery basketball
into our trash receptacle's
purple hoop.

2.

This sour one
needs honey.
I don't swab it on.
I bite in, make a face,
not missing a drop.

3.

My friend Aggie asked me what's
my favorite fruit. Grapefruit,
I say. She looks at me
like I'm a Walmart
and the line is ten people deep.

4.

Irma Thomas sang "a man is a
helluva thing." So is a grapefruit.
And a heavenly thing, too,
dropping from a California tree,
1,000 chimes in the rind.

5.

I told a grapefruit my deepest
secret—so far,
it hasn't blabbed. What if I carve it?
The silver knife digging deep,
my secret sliding off the counter and running.

Plan Without Lemons

At fourteen, I sat on Mrs. Acacia Perkins's
wooden steps and drank iced tea
without lemon. She said lemons
made the devil smile. I didn't ask,
didn't the devil need something
to smile about? It must be worse
than a Georgia summer in Hell,
or maybe just slightly better.

She said God had a plan for me:
minister. She patted my blond crew cut
as if I were Aladdin's lamp—
a great wish would burst out of me,
but my genies snuck away,
left no forwarding address. I pictured
my life as a minister. Ours wore
certainty like the black suit
he preached in. He chopped up doubt
to use for chicken feed. Having doubt,
I learned to be secretive—never admit it.
Be like a planter,
a spare house key buried
under a red geranium.

Her daughter Meg said that when
Mrs. Acacia Perkins died, her Bible
was open to Amos. The guys
took her away. We had lost touch.
I worked as a busboy, played guitar
in a throaty garage band, and preached
to a drum and a bass.

When I drink iced tea, I drop in lemon,
a giggle for the devil. I dig up my secrets,
display them like resale shop items.
Anything is worth a quarter. Here,
take something. I'm an open book.
You don't even have to read me.

Elegy for a Calamondin

Seven small fruits
hang on barren branches,

angry eyes. We should
apologize for not watering.
Instead, I make spaghetti,
watch TV. The oranges
thickened through summer,
even in fall. On Halloween
I took it in, gave it a sunny sill.

My spouse gets the vacuum cleaner,
sucks up leaves. He's both
funeral director and gravedigger.
Carrying it out,
he says nothing.

Hepatica

Picture Dusty singing
"Breakfast In Bed"
to Norma Tanega.
They touch tenderly
in places that Ed Sullivan
fears, the swingin' sixties
a time when even famous
heads get bashed
against a wall and
careers come down
with a terrible disease
and die of truth. Norma
puts her head on
Dusty's chest. The sun
has already gotten up
to make breakfast
for a hepatica blossom.

Trilliums

The trilliums have just
come into bloom,
raising little white flags
above brown fern fronds.

Why raise flags of surrender?
Each conquered winter.
These should be victory flags.

They see summer carrying
a large scythe. They know
they can't get out of the way.

They wait. They ask pebbles
for help, knowing how silent
pebbles are, how they
don't listen,
even to the Earth.

Yellow Buddleia

Even in tough winters,
the buddleia came through.

This March,
new shoots,
a good loaf of green
for the sun to slice into.
Three freezing days. By May,

branches snapped off.
I got the grub hoe and
slammed the roots,
making a circle until,
with much heaving,
the stump

gave way.

I tossed branches
in the can. The guys
flipped them into the truck
and drove away. Spring,

missing a yellow wing,
tried to fly and couldn't.

Fuschia

I tell few about Dun Dunt,
my invisible friend. He's fine
with that, says being a secret
makes him a man

of mystery. At four I met him.
At twenty he saw me through
my first affair—I'd like to say
romance, but love looked for
a parking spot while I loitered
in a lobby. Dun Dunt said
I'd survive. I did,
I guess.

If I look like a fuschia
that fell out of its pot,
Dun Dunt heads to the shed
for fresh dirt, snugs me in,
angles me in just
the right light.

I'm Misting

the orchids, exquisite but crabby: *Oh,
it has to be just the way
I like it*, the cattleya says. *No,
the way I like it*, the dendrobium says.

Loki flops in the Lazy Boy. Krishna
fixes a pot of tea. Athena shaves
her legs in my shower. I'd prefer
the gods to buzz off. Some prefer
to futz with us rather than with
each other—sometimes I don't
believe in orchids or gods,

yet there they are, demanding,
sometimes beautiful.

Planting in the Rain

A sudden rain. Stan hunts for
just the right place for
an elephant ear, a plant
like parking a van
in a green shoebox. I'm cutting down
old cassia canes. Maybe

as summer grows old, she'll sit
on our porch in a plastic chair—
fall

asleep in mid-sentence. Stan
and I will tiptoe back in the house,
listen to *The Supremes
Sing Holland Dozier Holland*
to drown out menacing steps
of autumn coming closer.

Blue Himalayan Poppy

Your logic won't impede me
this year—I'm ordering
a blue Himalayan poppy
which you say will surely die here
in sweaty Pennsylvania. What if

this blue Lazarus resurrects
to provide even a single blossom?
Sure, it would prefer living in
the Pacific Northwest. So would we,
but we can't drop our jobs off

like a stork dropping a bundle
on Washington. Blue petal waves
will find our yard's shoreline,
break and break all spring long.

Petunias

A visitor said, "Your petunias
look nice." Nice? These furies
can bite a leg off summer.

Rattlesnake petunias strike.
I walk by talking to myself and
WHAM—they go right for me.

With a petunia, everything is
a close call, a plot.
That bashful look, a ruse.
Put twenty together,
and it looks like peace
has laid down a picnic blanket.
Back off. There's no cure.

Once they get you,
you're done.

Weeding Borders

I tell myself: It's important
to have borders, even/especially
with those I love.

Like my garden, those borders
often fail. It starts imperceptibly—
the long phone call, the night
when work means I spend less time
with Stan. Things creep in, take
because I let them take.

This morning I noticed
two garden beds,
no borders left—grass
and weeds had slipped in:
how did I miss that?
I got on my knees and started
pulling, almost frantically. Creeping
charlie, some almost
three feet long, came out as I
cursed each strand. Tonight

I'm going to sit by Stan
and not talk about work,
neaten the border, make it
possible for beauty, slowly,
to come into blossom.

On Being Told Any Poet Who Writes About Flowers Is Safe

Flowers aren't safe or sweet.
That we give them to our
lovers for Valentine's Day
shows we are very sick
indeed. They'd steal from
your grandmother if they
could walk, demand a perfect
location or they sulk and die

angry. Flowers think our noses
are ugly planets falling
in their centers. As we ooh
and aah over their colors, they
mock our clothes and hate our

fingers which snap their necks off
and stuff stems in vases.
They train us to adore them
till it's the kiss-off when
winter becomes a corkscrew
for Earth's cold wine bottle.

In spring, each furious
thing reopens so we can stick
our faces close enough for them
to gouge our eyes out.

Giant Hogweed

You're walking out
in the country, nearly
bump into a huge plant,
maybe fourteen feet tall.
A castle, you want to enter it.
The roof is a flower
five feet wide. A single
touch

and your skin blisters,
looks like balloons grow
out of your bones. Get it
in your eyes and sight
gets sealed up for good.

You could have admired it
from a distance,
but you chose to enter.

Tragedy pops up.
Like a summer storm.
Sudden. Heavy rain
pummels you. Run.
You can't escape.

Popillia Japonica

Gold-shelled, you'd think these beetles
were royalty. When they congregate

on a Chicago peace rose,
their glamour fades. Criminals,
they thug petals. After I find
a cadaver stem where blossoms
had pinked the afternoon, I drop them
in a can of soapy water. Even then
they say *more, give me more,*

it's my right. A gold robe,
spun by death.

Rose After Eden

Bugs gnaw
on my petals. Soon my leaves
will go. I don't know what cold is,
but I fear it. Will the open sky
drop stuff on me? No protection.
On the ground, danger creeps
up from my roots. I had expected
to live forever. The people pluck

large leaves to wear, look afraid.
I've never seen that look before.
Thorns may defend me, but
as fierce as they are, I doubt
that they can. Only wither
will water me.

First Blossom

This dahlia
white paper
an ink well
in the center
a fairy dips
a wing
in the ink
draws   the wind
      unsure
   of where
to go next

A Red Dahlia

I remove my shoes, shirt,
and pants. Naked,
I step into the dahlia's bloom.
I'm late—our whole
neighborhood's already here.

We drink iced tea,
carve our initials
on sunlight,
share family recipes
with curious pebbles.

A Show-and-Tell Dahlia

The tuber has eyes
to see its way
into spring.

Only months ago,
reddish blossoms,
yellow tips,
like someone had
set the ends
on fire. The sun,
a struck match.

July: a strong stalk
more than waist-high
to hoist heavy blossoms.

The phone camera
makes each flower
look small, decorative.
Not the lion pacing
out of a bud
with a silent roar.

Belle of Barmera Dahlia

Blossoms blot out the full moon.
Even they must shrink back

into tubers that fit in my hand.
Each bloom tosses

one last pink spear
at November's turned back.

Sandia Rose Dahlia

A bay filled with water lilies
   yellow
        like the lake unwrapped
         a sun nugget
  and placed it on a lily pad.
While Jet Skis and pontoon boats
noise the quiet,

    the water
   lily drifts when
waves roll by
stems where minnows
see them as lampposts
  to lean on before
        darting away.

The Sandia Rose
dahlia has no bay

a garden bed is a kind of bay
the blossoms open to water
lily sized blooms that hover
    over the plant

I sip a morning
cup of coffee
seek a way to shrink myself
to enter a blossom
to become a minnow
swimming in mid-air
lavender petals
a sun buried within

here peace doesn't call us
by our names
we have no names
we float
it's delicious
if only for a few seconds.

I Like to See My Plants Naked

My Show-and-Tell dahlia
wears the most gorgeous black
cocktail dress made of night.
A firefly tiara tops off the ensemble.

This morning the garden
has the Show-and-Tell showing—
and telling. Stark naked in bright
lighting. Should I close my eyes

or turn my back? I don't.
If the dahlia's mellow
while being starkers in a suburb,
why should I care? I say
"My, your red and yellow
look like a lake at sunrise."

The blossom soon withers.
Like me.
All gone.
Only the ground
to take us in.

Adenium

August gets like a pair of raggedy shorts
that needs sewing despite the crocosmia's

orange blossoms. Torn rubber gloves
and a kinked hose

keep me from fully enjoying
the garden—until,

oh my, can it be, the adenium's tube
fully open, the first time

ever, red, so red, fabulously red,
giving time a color.

Tall Mexican Sunflowers

lean until they topple—

rope them up
to make them stand. Upright,
a single heavenly blue morning
glory at the top of the flagpole
looks down. A storm makes
mischief. Tithonias can't overcome
heavy rain and wind.

Morning: on the ground, uprooted,
yet dozens of blossoms
unharmed. Wind,

you can't still the orange
jamboree dancers, can't know
the orange dream that the sky
tells to fading clouds.

Farfugium with Exclamation Point

As August aches into September,
I cling to every remaining bloom,
some more fulsome than ever—
giant marigolds,
a red canna lily.
You'd think autumn was a rumor
easily disproved. October comes
more quickly than I imagined.
Aster time. Goldenrod.

November, I rub fading asters
and a roulette coreopsis
by the road. December,
the garden has closed its eyes
for the last time. Except—

a farfugium! Small daisy-like
yellow petals in a barrel
near the garage. On our way
to work, we see the flower tip
her hat to a gray sky, large
green leaves shining when
all hope seemed to go poof.

Moonflower on the Porch

I dream I'm with another man
who I meet in the Boscov's
furniture section
on a bubblegum-colored couch.

I say I already have a guy. He says
so what? Startled, I wake up,

you still sleeping. Life
gets normal again. Cats. Coffee.
The Dave Clark Five a needle drop away.
A late summer moonflower's
ghost on the porch.

November Potatoes

My trowel cuts a couple
in half, more joy
for the compost heap.
A stiff breeze makes me
want to return the tools
to the garage, drink tea
with Petula Clark.

Two things a garden teaches:
patience and discipline.

I unearth seven small potatoes.
November, withered beebalm
and zinnias, frost-scalded
toad lilies. This is the time

for Thanksgiving, for letting go,
the hardest thing, to let go
and still sing.

Start of Spring

Oh, magical
annoyance
that lives in
the sky—
we need you
to live, but

sometimes
I'd like to pull
down your yellow
pants
and spank you.

Today I need
a gray sky
with poufy hair
to block you.

Mask and Garden

At the grocery store, exhaling
fogs up my glasses. I miss Evelyn
the cashier's smile. She and I are
like two closed books. At home,

I take off the mask and visit
the garden. Our first Myrtle's Folly
dahlia has bloomed. Years of failure,
but this year, this rotten year,
a splendid blossom. Splendid
doesn't really say it. Sometimes
beauty has no language.
We must go in silence.

A new pink rose burst open.
I put my face into it. I head back
to our porch, a bright autumn
sun zigzagging
from orchid to orchid.

Ghost Garden

I walk past the garden bed
where we released
my mother's ashes.
Two cats are buried there.
Sunflowers and pink rogersia
thrive where death
makes a home. Sometimes
by a light of fireflies,
I think I see my mom
and those cats. The moon
reddens above the roof,
and every year
flowers return.

Title Index

A

Adam, a Week Before Dying 39
Adenium 75
A Hiker 22
Antique Store Bette Davis 26
A Red Dahlia 69
A Show-and-Tell Dahlia 70

B

Belle of Barmera Dahlia 71
Bloody Mary 45
Blue Himalayan Poppy 61

C

Chester, 12, Looks in the Mirror 28
Cold Tapioca 29
Cowardly Lion Now 36

D

Dad's Science 19

E

Elegy for a Calamondin 54

F

Farfugium with Exclamation Point 77
First Blossom 68
First Pansies 49
Found Picture 17
Fuschia 58

G

Genesis Unexpurgated 40
Geometry Teacher 32
Ghost Garden 82
Giant Hogweed 65
Grace by the Piano 20
Grapefruit 50

H

Hades Wants It All the Time 44
Hector Husband 15
Hepatica 55
Hopkins in Doubt 35

I

I Like to See My Plants Naked 74
I'm Misting 59
I Visit Moma and Lunch with Frank O'Hara 16

J

Judas Upgraded 41

L

Loki 42
Lovable Moptops 21

M

Marriage and Canned Peaches 18
Mars Changing Her Name 24
Mask and Garden 81
Medusa and Men 43
Men in Eve's Life 37
Moonflower on the Porch 78
My Sister Agatha Can Fly 14

N

New Seed Catalogues 48
November Potatoes 79

O

Old Salt 30
On Being Told Any Poet Who Writes
    About Flowers Is Safe 64

P

Petunias 62
Planting in the Rain 60
Plan Without Lemons 52
Pompeii 31
Popillia Japonica 66
Post-Donald 33
Promises, Promises 27

R

Rose After Eden 67

S

Sandia Rose Dahlia 72
Start of Spring 80

T

Talking About Hinduism with Thoreau 25
Talking Snake 38
Tall Mexican Sunflowers 76
The Drop In 23
Trilliums 56

W

Weeding Borders 63
Woodrow Wilson 46

Y

Yellow Buddleia 57

First Line Index

A

A barren lilac 17
A bay filled with water lilies 72
After we broke up, Donald met a reporter 33
A picture of Mary's bleeding 18
As August aches into September 77
A sudden rain. Stan hunts for 60
At fourteen, I sat on Mrs. Acacia Perkins's 52
A trickster, I dwell in surprise 42
At the foot of my boyhood bed 15
At the grocery store, exhaling 81
August gets like a pair of raggedy shorts 75
A visitor said, "Your petunias 62

B

Blossoms blot out the full moon 71
Bugs gnaw 67

C

Cornflake sky falls into a bowl 16

D

Dad called her a princess 14
Dante's betrayers faced horror 41
Dear Dionne Warwick, that champagne 27
Did Eve find the snake's 38
discovers a skeleton 22

E

Even in tough winters 57

F

Flowers aren't safe or sweet 64
For my ninth birthday 46
From the tops of stairs 43

G

Gold-shelled, you'd think these beetles 66
Grace would come over for coffee 20
Grandma calls me *pudgy* 28

H

Hades wants it all the time. I think 44
He complains endlessly about how tired he is 37
Heretics 45
His integers got me 19

I

I dream I'm with another man 78
I got named after a war god 24
I love a man, Lord, and don't know 35
I pluck leaves 48
I quit Oz after eight months 36
I remove my shoes, shirt 69
I riffle through photos 26
I saw them first on Ed Sullivan 21

I tell few about Dun Dunt 58
I tell myself: It's important 63
I've always taught that the shortest distance 32
I've spent my life blaming her 39
I walk past the garden bed 82

L

lean until they topple 76

M

My Show-and-Tell dahlia 74
My trowel cuts a couple 79

O

of the year! A flat for twenty bucks 49
Oh, magical 80
On the first day 40

P

Picture Dusty singing 55

S

Seven small fruits 54
Squirt me in the eye again 50

T

the orchids, exquisite but crabby: Oh 59
The trilliums have just 56
The tuber has eyes 70
This dahlia 68

W

We ask to take his picture 30
When I told Dun Dunt that 29
When I visit his little grave 25
When Li Bei drops in, and normally 23

Y

Your beauty is like a calendar 31
You're walking out 65
Your logic won't impede me 61

www.ingramcontent.com/pod-product-compliance
Lightning Source LLC
Chambersburg PA
CBHW010046090426
42735CB00020B/3406